NESSIE

The Legend of the Loch Ness Monster

Betty Kirkpatrick

Crombie Jardine
PUBLISHING LIMITED

Unit 17, 196 Rose Street, Edinburgh EH2 4AT
www.crombiejardine.com

This edition was first published by Crombie Jardine Publishing Limited in 2005

ISBN 1-905102-05-4

Designed by www.mrstiffy.co.uk
Printed and bound in the United Kingdom by
William Clowes, Beccles, Suffolk

CONTENTS

INTRODUCTION

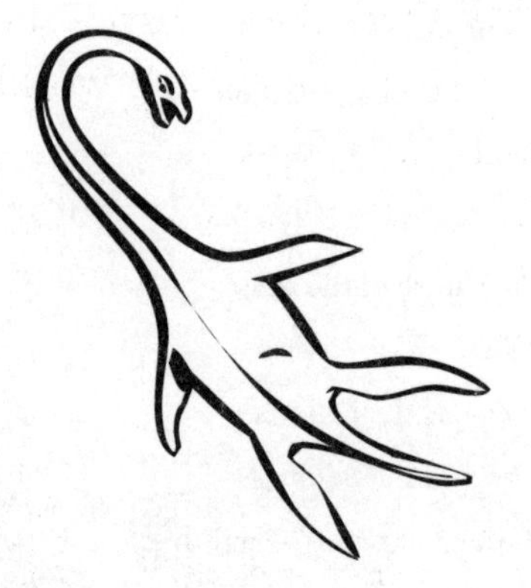

Historically, Scotland has had many famous sons. Over the centuries she has given to the world more than her fair share of engineers, explorers, inventors, doctors, writers, captains of industry and so on.

Alas, famous daughters have not been nearly so thick on the ground. They were far too busy giving birth to and rearing the famous sons to spare the time to grab a piece of the fame for themselves.

However, it is just possible that one day the Scottish female sex will get its revenge for all this neglect. One of their number could have the potential to achieve far more fame than

any of the males so far. Indeed, she is already very widely known.

The only trouble is that we don't know whether she actually exists or not. I refer, of course, to Nessie, more formally and more fearsomely known as the Loch Ness Monster.

Nessie is the pet name given to a creature that may, or may not, live within the waters of Loch Ness in the Scottish Highlands. She has been the subject of great controversy for years. Some believe in her implicitly; others think she is at best a myth, and at worst a load of old codswallop.

WHAT'S IN A NAME?

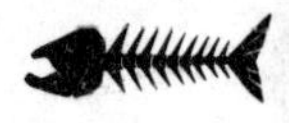

It seems over-familiar, and rather disrespectful, to use a nickname such as Nessie to refer to the ultra-large potential inhabitant of Loch Ness, especially when no-one has been introduced to her. Still, she is no stranger to disrespect.

We have only to think of the many souvenirs that are sold in her supposed image, some of a violent green colour and sporting tartan berets.

No wonder Nessie chooses to
hide herself away!

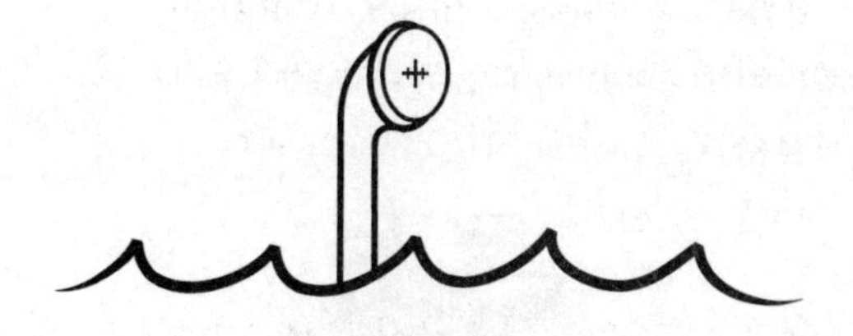

Her more imposing title, the Loch Ness Monster, was supposedly given to her by Dr Evan Barron, editor of *The Inverness Courier*, when a sighting was reported in his newspaper in 1933.

But 'monster' is a frightening kind of word with many unpleasant associations and, in time, the creature of Loch Ness was brought down to size, so to speak, and became known to all and sundry as Nessie.

In the early 1970s she was given a title that was even grander than the Loch Ness Monster. Sir Peter Scott,

the famous and well-respected British naturalist, and, unlike many other members of the scientific establishment, a firm believer in the existence of Nessie, gave her the Latin name of *Nessiteras rhombopteryx*.

This has been translated as 'Ness

wonder with a diamond-shaped fin', the reference to such a fin having arisen because of an underwater photograph taken in 1972, by one of a team headed by Dr Robert Rines of the American Academy of Applied Sciences.

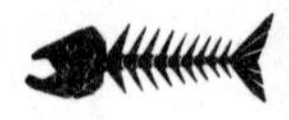

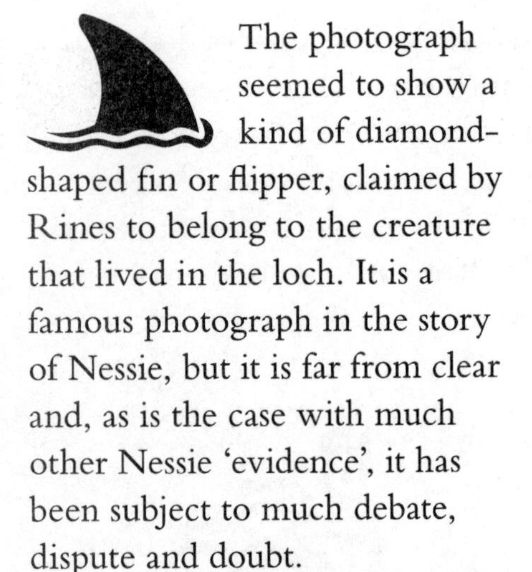

The photograph seemed to show a kind of diamond-shaped fin or flipper, claimed by Rines to belong to the creature that lived in the loch. It is a famous photograph in the story of Nessie, but it is far from clear and, as is the case with much other Nessie 'evidence', it has been subject to much debate, dispute and doubt.

Sir Peter Scott was perhaps just

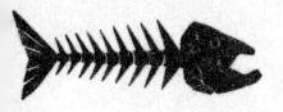

trying to get Nessie a bit of status and credibility by giving her a Latin name. After all, most other creatures have a classical alternative to their everyday description. However, there were many who refused to take either the name or his belief in Nessie seriously.

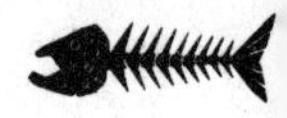

One sceptic pointed out that *Nessiteras rhombopteryx* is an anagram of 'monster hoax by Sir Peter S'.

Even that is not the end of Nessie's naming problems. Some of Nessie's supporters dislike the word 'monster', preferring to use the term 'unknown animal', in some ways, even more of a comedown than Nessie. Still, the renaming was done out of the best possible motives.

They thought that the term monster smacked too much of mythology and that its use detracted from Nessie's credibility as a bona fide inhabitant of Loch Ness.

Dignity was restored once again when it was suggested that Nessie should be dubbed a cryptid.

By this time the search for Nessie had been given the grand-sounding name of cryptozoology rather than monster-hunting. Derived from the Greek word *kruptos*, hidden, cryptozoology is the study of creatures, such as Nessie, whose existence has not been scientifically proven. A cryptid is such a creature.

LOCATION, LOCATION, LOCATION

As any estate agent will tell you, when it comes to accommodation, location is all-important. Nessie, if she exists, has obviously taken this message to heart. Believed to be so retiring that she makes even Garbo appear gregarious, she has chosen the perfect place for her hideaway.

Loch Ness, which in England would be called a lake, is extremely deep, so deep, indeed,

that it could cover some of the tallest buildings in the world. Its depth is variable and difficult to measure, but it is said to be nearly 1,000 feet deep in places, with an average depth of around 750 feet.

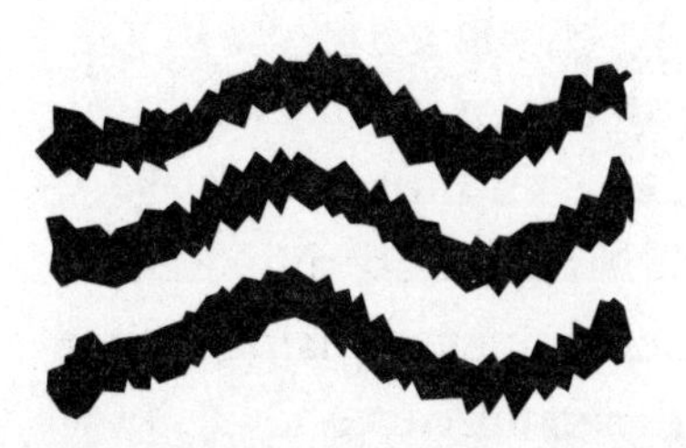

The loch's length, too, is impressive, since it measures 24 miles long and is the largest stretch of fresh water in the British Isles. Nessie obviously likes a lot of personal space.

It has long been held by some Nessie believers that the depth of Loch Ness is made even more attractive for a large creature intent on concealment by the presence of underwater caves.

People in favour of this theory believe that these are too deep and dark to be explored even by modern scientific methods. Since such caves have not been proved to exist, sceptics have been quick to assume that they do not. However, believers in the cave theory were given a bit of a boost in the early 1990s, when an auxiliary coastguard and local businessman,

George Edwards, identified a large circular depression in the loch floor near Urquhart Bay. Members of the caves school of thought were convinced that this discovery represented an access point to underwater caverns and so was Nessie's likely home.

Non-believing experts pooh-poohed this, and suggested instead that the depression was a result of some previous underwater seismic activity.

The suggestion that Nessie has another underwater hideaway in the form of a tunnel which links Loch Ness to the sea is much less likely.

The loch is about 52 feet above sea level. Loch Ness also provides

another aid to privacy as well as space and depth. The presence of peat in the loch, brought down into it from feeder streams and the river, makes the water rather brown and murky.

The particles of peat floating about in it hinder visibility even further for those peering into the loch, hoping for a glimpse of its supposed giant occupant.

Add to this the fact that, even today, the views of Loch Ness

from the roads along it are often obstructed by trees and bushes and you must admit that Nessie chose her habitat well. Good as they are, however, her conditions are not so ideal as they once were.

In 1933 a Class A road was completed along the north shore of the loch, giving access to cars and affording vastly improved opportunities for monster-sighting. Rocks were blasted away, and extensive areas of woodland cleared in the course of the road-building, making Nessie much more vulnerable to prying eyes.

SIGHTINGS

There have been far too many claimed sightings of Nessie, even those which have in some way been officially recorded, to mention any but a few of them here.

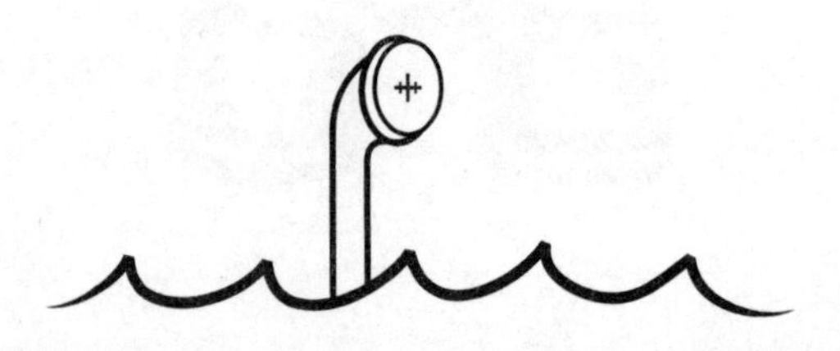

The first written report of a Ness monster appeared many centuries before the new road of 1933 in a biography of St Columba written by Adamnan, the Abbott of Iona.

The account claims that in 565 Columba encountered a group of people on the banks of the River Ness in the act of burying a friend who had been fatally bitten by a water monster while he was swimming.

The monster is then said to have tried to attack one of Columba's men when he was swimming to the other side of the river to collect a boat.

At this point, according to the biography, Columba made a sign of the cross and ordered the monster to retreat. The monster duly obeyed the order.

But this could be construed as the stuff of legend. Nessie's modern fame really began in the spring of 1933 with a report in *The Inverness Courier*, Nessie's local paper.

This told how Mr and Mrs John Mackay were driving from Inverness along the loch to Drumnadrochit, where they ran the local hotel, when Mrs Mackay noticed a disturbance in the loch,

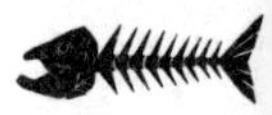

and asked her husband to pull up.

The article claimed that the Mackays observed something very large and with two black humps rise from the water before descending again.

This report not only saw the start of a rush of other sightings, but it was also the signal for several people to mention much earlier sightings claimed to have been made by themselves or by relatives or friends.

It is not all that surprising that local people would have kept quiet about such sightings. Being Celts, their silence might have owed as much to superstition or to a belief in the supernatural as

to a general taciturnity or to a desire not to appear foolish. Some of them might even have had in mind the long-standing legend of the kelpies, evil spirits who supposedly took the form of water horses and waited by riverbanks or loch sides to lure people to their deaths.

Before more supposed facts were available about Nessie, people may well have thought that they had seen a kelpie instead of the Loch Ness monster, especially since the kelpie could supposedly change shape.

The majority of alleged modern sightings have been of Nessie in the water, but a famous land sighting took place not long after the Mackays' water sighting described earlier, and the report

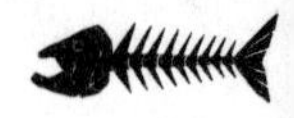

of this increased even further the interest in Nessie and the number of claimed views of her.

On 22 July 1933, Mr and Mrs George Spicer from London were driving south from John O'Groats along the east shore of the loch, when they claimed to have seen what appeared to be some kind of prehistoric animal.

Spicer described it in a letter to *The Inverness Courier* as having a large, greyish, high-backed, body and a long neck 'which moved up and down in the manner of a scenic railway' with something, possibly its folded-back tail, flapping up and down where the neck and body joined. The body was estimated to be about 25 feet in length and the neck 6–8 feet and the creature was

described as carrying something, possibly a lamb, in its mouth.

The year 1933 was a good year for Nessie's PR. As well as the sightings already mentioned here, there was another extremely noteworthy event in that publication of the first photograph of an alleged Nessie sighting took place. It was taken on 12 November by Hugh Gray, a worker with the British Aluminium Company, and appeared to show the greyish body of a large creature surrounded by a great deal of spray.

The photograph is far from clear and, as with many photographs of alleged Nessie sightings, there have been suggestions either that it has been touched up or that it is a fake. It has been alleged, for example, that the photograph is, in fact, of the head of a Labrador dog with a stick in its mouth.

These were milestone events in the history of Nessie.

A great many people ranging from lone watchers on the shore to photographers laden with state-of-the-art cameras and researchers armed with the latest hi-tech sonar equipment have done their best to see and identify Nessie. As yet, she has defied all of their attempts.

APPEARANCE

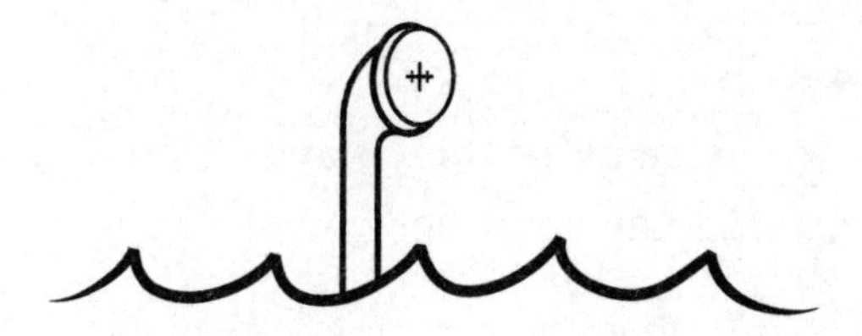

As you can imagine, it is difficult to give an Identikit picture of a creature whose very existence is open to doubt. Nevertheless, there have been thousands of claimed sightings of Nessie and a good many of these have given a similar description.

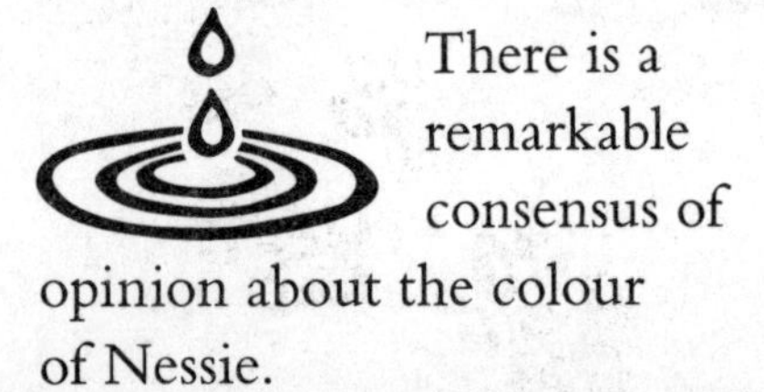

There is a remarkable consensus of opinion about the colour of Nessie.

As befits a creature who
shies away from the limelight,
Nessie is said to be of a shade
that blends in well with her
surroundings. Thus, she is
supposedly dark grey
or dark brown,
good camouflage
colours for
Loch Ness.

Those who claim to have seen Nessie are not in such harmony when it comes to the texture of her skin. Some have described it as rather oily or shiny, while others have claimed it is of a scaly appearance.

At least since the sightings from the 1930s on, it is usually agreed by Nessie-spotters that she has a very long neck and probably rather a small head.

Some descriptions have added a pair of small horns to the head. Others have added a long, lashing tail to the other end.

The estimated length of Nessie is subject to a degree of variability, but from the wealth of descriptions given by those who claimed to have seen her, she is generally held to be about 30–40 feet in length. Whatever her exact measurements, she is very big... if she exists, of course.

However, her great size does not prevent her from moving very fast apparently, for many commentators have referred to her great speed in the water. Estimates of up to 30 miles per hour have been claimed, a speed that results in Nessie leaving a substantial wash behind her.

One thing unites most descriptions of Nessie. The

majority of the alleged observers indicate that Nessie has the hump. Indeed, she is often described as having more than one hump, as many as seven having been mentioned.

On water Nessie is said to undulate sinuously, but on land her gait is far from elegant. There have been far fewer reported land

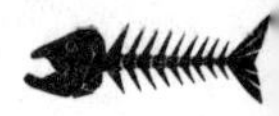

sightings than water sightings, but those that exist point to a rather lumbering creature, some descriptions mentioning very small feet.

THE NATURE OF THE BEAST

In modern times at least, we have little reason to believe that Nessie, should she really be living in Loch Ness, is particularly savage or dangerous, at least as far as humans are concerned. Certainly we do not hear reports of her suddenly making off with any of the people who are trying to

capture her on camera. Instead, she appears to be a shy, retiring creature, who makes very few appearances and who quickly makes herself scarce if she is spotted.

Yet, she is described by some of those who claimed to have had a sight of her on land as being very fierce in appearance, and at least one account describes her as having some kind of animal in her mouth.

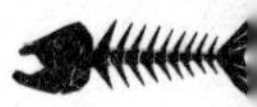

Her very size is, of course, somewhat intimidating, and tends to ensure that anyone who did encounter her on land would not be likely to stay around long enough to assess the nature of her temperament.

WHAT'S THERE?

There are many people who believe implicitly that there is some kind of large, albeit unknown, creature in Loch Ness.

On the other hand, there are many people who dismiss the whole idea as being ridiculous, despite the large number of claimed sightings of such a creature.

THE VIEWS OF THE BELIEVERS

Most scientists in Britain, like most politicians, have shied away from expressing any definite belief in the existence of an ultra-large, strange creature in Loch Ness. The whole thing sounds so unlikely and the establishment generally has a horror of being made to look foolish.

One of the few members of the establishment who did throw his weight behind Nessie, and

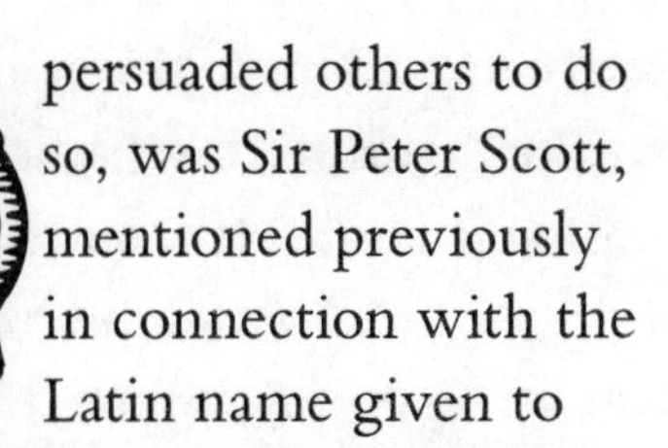

persuaded others to do so, was Sir Peter Scott, mentioned previously in connection with the Latin name given to Nessie. He helped to found the Loch Ness Investigation Bureau in the early 1960s, the aim of this being to conduct systematic research on the loch.

Scott came to be of the opinion that the creature that he believed to inhabit Loch Ness was a plesiosaur. This was a prehistoric, fish-eating reptile whose appearance bore a significant resemblance to that frequently attributed to Nessie. It had, for example, a long neck, a small head and a long tail. Furthermore, it was known to exist in Britain.

This is a popular theory, not least because, even before the film *Jurassic Park*, many people had an interest in, and even a soft spot for, prehistoric creatures. The rather romantic notion that there could be one living in Loch Ness captured the nation's imagination.

Alas, for this theory, the timing is all wrong. There is the inconvenient fact that the plesiosaur is thought to have died out around 70 million

years ago. Even this does not deter those who put their faith in the plesiosaur or some other prehistoric species that is living in a time warp in Loch Ness.

Their faith is bolstered by the fact that, in 1938, a coelacanth, a kind of carnivorous fish, was caught alive off the coast of Africa. 'What is the connection with Nessie?' you might well ask.

Well, the coelacanth, like the plesiosaur, was also thought to have died out 70 million year ago. If the coelacanth was alive and swimming, why should a plesiosaur not inhabit Loch Ness?

One answer is that we are back to location again. Loch Ness is nowhere near as old as the plesiosaur and so it is difficult to understand how one or, more likely, several of them could be skulking there. Indeed,

Ness is not much more than 10,000 years old, not having come into being until the end of the last Ice Age.

Implicit believers in the plesiosaur theory like to believe that the creature was in Loch Ness when the land rose after the melting of the ice and the loch was cut off from the sea, although experts in these matters have written this off.

Another theory has it that the plesiosaur accidentally swam up the River Ness, which rises in Loch Ness and flows into the sea, and took up residence in the loch.

This is decidedly unlikely, since the River Ness is quite shallow

and a very large creature would
have difficulty navigating it,
especially without being seen.

Then there is the temperature of the location. The plesiosaur, being a reptile, was cold-blooded and so relied on its surroundings to warm it up to a survival temperature. It was a marine animal and thus used to the warmish waters of the sea. Loch Ness is very cold, although it never freezes over, and is not at all a suitable habitat for this prehistoric creature.

The plesiosaur theory is related to an earlier idea that Nessie is a sea serpent, but this proposal gets us precisely nowhere. The sea serpent, you see, is just as much a cryptid, or unknown animal, as Nessie.

Although, over the centuries, there have been many people who believed in such a phenomenon and some who claimed to have seen one, there is no scientific proof of its existence and there is even more scepticism associated with the sea serpent than there is with Nessie. An early edition of Chambers Twentieth-Century Dictionary is exceptionally dismissive of the sea serpent, defining it as

'an enormous marine animal of serpent-like form frequently seen and described by credulous sailors, imaginative landsmen and common liars'.

Even if the dictionary is proved wrong and a sea serpent does show up one day, it is not at all certain that Nessie would turn out to be such a creature.

The problem would remain as to how such a huge sea creature got to Loch Ness in the first place and then succeeded in surviving in what was, to it, an alien environment.

The problem for Nessie believers is that her suggested appearance, even without the variations from sighting to sighting, does not really relate to any known species.

However, this does not deter the more fervent of Nessie fans, some believing that Nessie might either be one of an as yet unknown species and others that she is an exceptionally large version of some known species that has adapted to the environment of Loch Ness in some odd way.

Some ultra-large version of a mammal has been suggested, but, if this were the case, many more sightings would be expected. Mammals need to surface in order to breathe and we would expect them to come on land much more frequently, at least to breed. It would be cruel to assume that Nessie is a lonely celibate

who has outlived the rest of her clan by thousands of years.

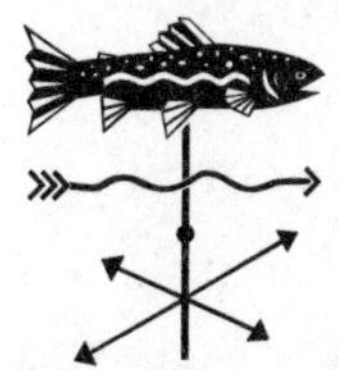

Several people are now of the opinion that the supposed dweller in Loch Ness is some kind of giant fish. Some species of fish dwell on the bottom of the sea, but come up to the surface occasionally when the weather is warm and calm.

Such a habit ties in well with the fact that Nessie-sightings are far from being an everyday occurrence and that they do seem to have a tendency to occur in fine weather.

Furthermore, the discovery of an exceptionally old and large sturgeon, mentioned in the section to follow, put some weight behind the fish theory.

However, there are other problems, a major one of these being the question of physical appearance. Nessie's reported long thin neck and small head certainly do not instantly call to mind a fish.

THE VIEWS OF THE DOUBTERS

Disbelievers have proved very adept at coming up with rational explanations for the supposed sightings of Nessie. Many have suggested that the sightings have, in fact, been of creatures which do live in that habitat, and which have been either larger in size than the usual specimens, although nothing like as large as claimed, or have

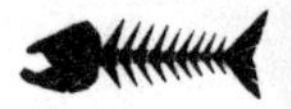

appeared so to the watcher, because of some trick of the light or water.

For example, it has been suggested that the claimed monster of Loch Ness is nothing other than a seal. Grey seals can apparently grow to a much larger size than we are used to and their movement in water can create such a wash that watchers might well over-estimate their size. It is true that seals have been observed in the River Ness, which runs from Loch Ness to the sea.

Other wildlife suggestions include otters, on the grounds that they, although usually only about three or four feet in length, can appear to be much longer when they are swimming. Furthermore, the otter-fanciers say otters can

swim very fast and when an otter is rising to the surface it appears to have a long neck of the kind attributed to Nessie. Some kind of giant eel has been also suggested, but, although there are eels in Loch Ness, none has ever been caught that comes anywhere near Nessie's supposed size.

A very large sturgeon is a popular proposition, this being the largest type of fish to be found in a fresh-water habitat. A significant degree of credibility was added to this idea when a sturgeon 11 feet in length and estimated to be over 80 years old, was found

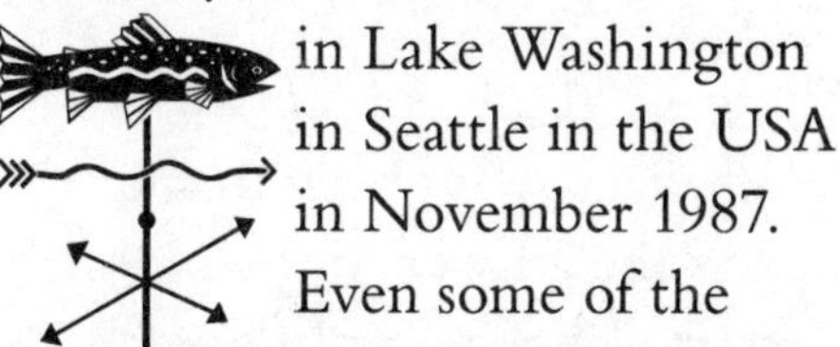

in Lake Washington in Seattle in the USA in November 1987. Even some of the

Nessie believers thought that this was possibly a relative of Nessie.

There are those doubters who favour deer swimming in the loch as the answer to the Nessie mystery. They point to the fact

that deer do swim and, with their long necks, could appear from the distance, especially in conditions of poor visibility, to resemble descriptions of Nessie. In addition, young deer have short un-branched antlers that could account for the horns that some Nessie-spotters have mentioned.

Nessie has also been declared to be nothing more than a flock of birds or a shoal of fish.

It has been suggested, for example, that from the side a line of swimming geese could be thought to resemble a series of humps, such as are frequently mentioned in descriptions of Nessie. As for the fish,

exceptionally large shoals of them have been cited as likely explanations for the remarkably

large underwater objects which
sonar equipment has recorded.

Others look no further than
the water itself for a rational
explanation of the Nessie enigma,
especially since Loch Ness
can become very stormy in an
amazingly short space of time.
Some doubters think that the
formation of waves
could mislead some
people into thinking
that this might, in

fact, be the form of a monster, bearing in mind that waves undulate in the way that Nessie is often claimed to do.

Others have suggested that waterspouts, long, tapering, funnels of water sucked up by the clouds, might have suggested a creature with a long neck to watchers on the shore.

A proposal made very recently by an Italian professor, Luigi

Piccardi, has it that the mighty Nessie is nothing more substantial than a series of gas bubbles coming to the surface of Loch Ness and creating the kind of commotion often attributed to the activities of Nessie. Supposedly, the said gas bubbles are a result of the remnants of the seismic activity that caused the fault known as the Great Glen that cuts across the Highlands of Scotland.

Low clouds and shadows cast on the loch by trees, etc., or a combination of these have also been used as plausible explanations for Nessie-spotting. The weather, as so often in Scotland, has come in for its share of the blame. In the Nessie situation the weather simply cannot win.

On fine days responsibility for Nessie-sighting is

ascribed to sunlight on the water causing a kind of mirage. On duller days responsibility is ascribed to mist and rain affecting visibility and causing people to see things imprecisely and so misinterpret them.

A considerable number of Nessie sceptics are in favour of boat wakes being the explanation.

Often, Nessie seems to choose calm days to appear to watchers and the wash from boats can look bigger and stay around much longer when there are no stormy winds or turbulent waves to break them up.

Opponents of this theory point to the fact that, although there are many vessels on Loch Ness, in many claimed sightings there were no

boats anywhere near at the time.

Floating vegetation has also been blamed for the Nessie sightings, although, by the very nature of the loch, there is not much in the way of plant growth in it. Still, there is plenty of woodland around and logs, branches, and even tree trunks, which have sunk below the surface, have been put forward as explanations of Nessie sightings.

Doubters have worked hard at accounting for the many claimed sightings of Nessie and several of these have been considerably more bizarre than any of those mentioned here. One suggestion has it that a German airship fell into the loch during World War 1 and occasionally bobs to the surface.

Another suggestion, made as recently as 1992 by a radiologist, Paul Goddard, surmises that

Nessie might be an elephant, presumably one that had somehow gained its freedom from a zoo or circus.

No one has admitted to such a loss and an elephant is unlikely to take kindly to a life under water.

Then there is the proposal that what people are mistaking for a monster in Loch Ness is simply a dummy of one. This is not quite so ludicrous as it sounds because, in 1969, a dummy was constructed to resemble the popular image of Nessie. The plan was to attach the dummy to a submarine, called *Pisces*, which would tow it around part of the loch where sightings were most common.

Presumably the hope was that the real Nessie would be curious about what was going on and pop to the surface for a peek. Alas, for the researchers, the towing cable broke and the dummy drifted free and then sank.

The dummy theory, of course, conveniently forgets that the dummy only existed because Nessie was thought to do so.

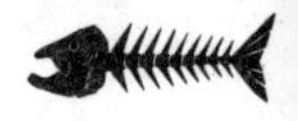

And what about the thousands of sightings that took place before 1969?

One of the most outlandish suggestions to date is reported to have come from John Erik Beckjord, an American wildlife photographer, who filmed video footage of Loch Ness in 1983. One photograph showed a moving object producing a wake and another seems to show

three large dark objects moving off together. Beckjord claimed that these photographs were respectively Nessie and three other monsters that must also inhabit the loch.

A few years later, in 1991, he is credited with writing an article suggesting that space travellers might have paid Loch Ness a visit and lost some of their pets, leaving

them in the loch when they returned home. Thus, Nessie could be part of a real-life Star Wars situation just longing for a space ship to turn up and take her home.

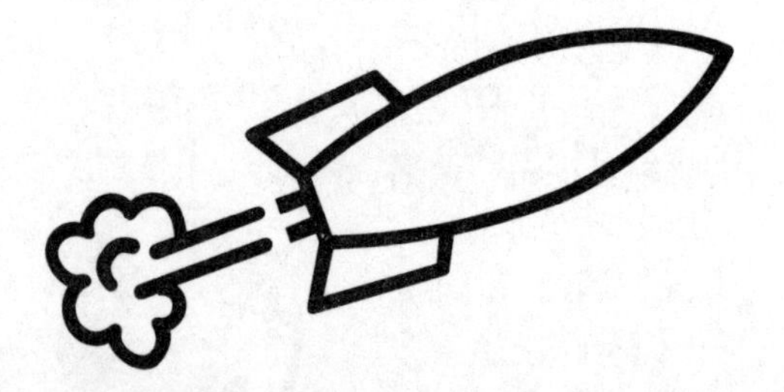

These, then are some of the suggestions that have been put forward to account for the Nessie sightings. However, many sceptics are of the opinion that the sightings are mostly the result of a fevered imagination or of hallucination, sometimes brought on by something else that Scotland is famous for...

whisky.

They are no more impressed by supposed photographic evidence of Nessie's existence than they are by alleged sightings, claiming that many such photographs are either so unclear as to be valueless or have been touched up or enhanced in some way. Others they claim to be hoaxes and there have, in truth, been several hoaxes, photographic and otherwise, uncovered in the course of the Nessie story.

One such photograph is that popularly known as 'the surgeon's photograph', this being a reference to the profession of Lieutenant-Colonel Robert Wilson who took the photograph.

This, which seems to show a creature with a long neck and small head, was once heralded as conclusive evidence that there was, indeed, a monster in Loch Ness.

However, it is now generally believed to be a fake, not least because in 1994 the photographer Christopher Spurling confessed to a friend that he had put together a hoax by placing a plastic model

of a neck and head on a toy submarine and sending it out on to the loch. This, he said, was the subject of the surgeon's photograph.

So there you have it: a summary of the case for and against Nessie. You will have to decide for yourself which camp you are going to support. Alternatively, you could join me on the fence.

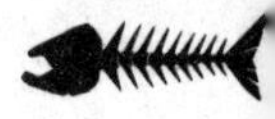

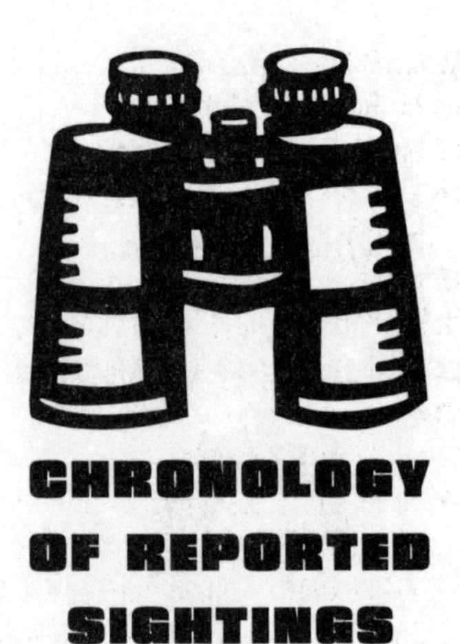

CHRONOLOGY OF REPORTED SIGHTINGS

1871 Mr D Mackenzie
1885 Mr Roderick Matheson
1888 Mr Alexander Macdonald
1895 Salmon Angler, Forester, Hotel Keeper and Fishing Ghillies
1908 Mr John Macleod
1923 Mr William Miller and D McGillvray
1929 Mrs Cumming and D McGillvray
1930 Mr Ian J Milne
1932 Mr James Cameron
1933 Mr and Mrs Mackay; Mr and Mrs George Spicer; Mr Hugh Gray; Mr Alexander Shaw and Mr Alister Shaw; Miss N Smith; Miss P Keyes, RAR Meiklem and Mrs Meiklem; Mr AH Palmer; Mr G McQueen; Mr John Cameron; Mrs E Garden Scott; Mrs B McDonell and Mrs Sutherland;

Mr WDH Moir; Mrs J Simpson; Mr A Gillies; Miss C MacDonald; Mr C Macrae and Mr J Mackinnon; Miss N Simpson; Mr G Jamieson

1934 Mr Howard Carson; Mrs M MacLennan; Mr William Mackay; Mr William Mackay and Mr William Campbell; Mr RJ Scott; Mr J Mackintosh; Mr A Ross; Mr D Ralph; Mr P Grant and Mr James Legge; Mr RJ Scott and Mr Evan Strang; Sir Murdock MacDonald and 2 others

1936 Mrs Marjory Moir and 4 others

1943 CB Farrel

1947 Mr and Mrs Donald MacIver and 3 others

1956 Mr and Mrs Alan Graham

1960 Mr Peter O'Connor; Mr Bruce Ing; Rev

and Mrs WL Dobb and son

1961 Mr McIntosh and Mr Cameron

1963 Mr Alastair Grant and Mr Ayton

1964 Peter and Pauline Hodge

1965 Miss EMJ Keith and James T Ballantyne; FW Holiday, William Fraser and John Cameron; Edward and Vivianne Elliott

1966 Mr and Mrs Alistair Macdonald; Mr and Mrs Pommitz; Mae Macdonald and Sylvia Paterson; B M Cameron and niece; FS Young; Lena Holmgren; RW Swan; Heather Cary and Mother; Angela Veitch

1967 David Wathen; Peter Davies; Norman Schofield; Dennis Gartrell; Dennis Bland; John Stroud

1968 Miss C Sanders; Philip Bull and

Howard Pratt; Cmdr RK Silcock and Mrs Silcock; JFM MacLeod

1969 Bruce Marshall and Bill Jobes; Mr and Mrs D Clayton and Mr and Mrs Maurice Smith; RA Moyse, two sons and a friend; Mr and Mrs Geoffrey Craven and 2 children

1973 Mr Jenkyns

1979 Paul H. Biermasz

1996 Bill Kinder; Staff at Craigdarroch House Hotel; Emilio Demnio and Nikhi Bayeri; Nick Watson and two others; Craig Kerr; Frank Meyer

1998 Adam and Mark Sutherland, Peter Gillies and Peter Rhind

NESSIE-SPOTTING DIARY

Keep this book handy at all times when visiting Loch Ness. Please be sure, if you do spot Nessie, to get the details down and – this is most important

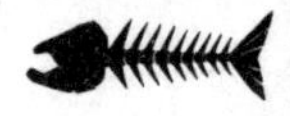

– get corroboration from a friend or a member of the public who witnessed the event with you. Take it immediately to the local police station – along with your witness – and have the policeman co-sign the sighting and confirm that you and your witness are both of sound mind.

LOCH NESS POLICE STATIONS

Depending on where you are when you see Nessie, please go to one of the following police stations.

(North of the Loch)
Inverness Police Station
Inverness
IV1 1AD
☎ 01463 715555

(Middle of the Loch)
Drumnadrochit Police Station
Drumnadrochit
IV3 6TX
☎ 01456 450222

(End of the Loch)
Fort Augustus Police Station
Fort Augustus
PH32 4BH
☎ 01320 366222

After contacting the police, get in touch with the news editor at
The Inverness Courier
New Century House
Stadium Road
Inverness
IV1 1FF
☎ 01463 233059

If you have a photograph to back up your sighting, do not – on any account – sign this over to the first person that asks for it.

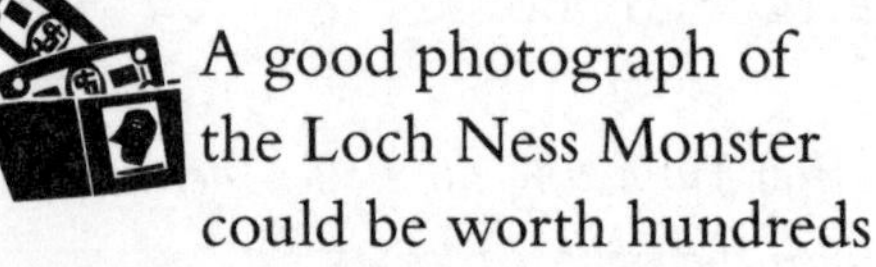

A good photograph of the Loch Ness Monster could be worth hundreds of thousands of pounds to you and you should seek legal advice before signing any contract.

Date	Time	Amount of whisky consumed	Description of the wee beastie	Witnesses

INDEX

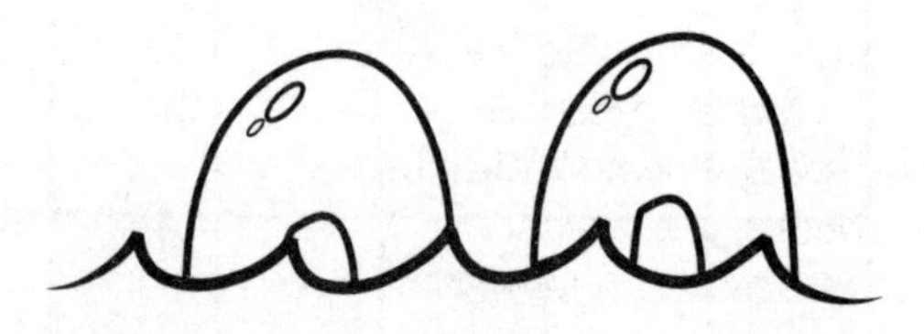

Crombie Jardine books are available from
High Street bookshops, Amazon or
Bookpost
P.O.Box 29
DOUGLAS
ISLE OF MAN
IM99 1BQ

Tel. 01624 677237
Fax. 01624 670923
Email: bookshop@enterprise.net
(Postage and packing free within the UK)

GREYFRIARS BOBBY

ISBN: 1-905102-04-6

105x85mm, 128pp, pb, £2.99

SCOTTISH WIT & WISDOM

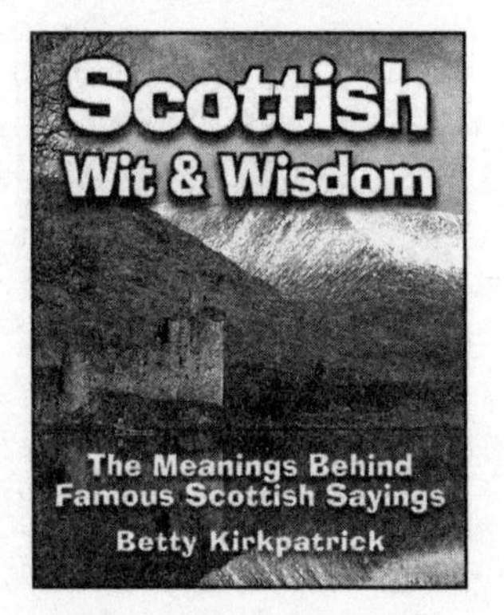

ISBN: 1-905102-07-0

105x85mm, 128pp, pb, £2.99

AULD SCOTTISH GRANNIES' REMEDIES

ISBN: 1-905102-06-2

105x85mm, 128pp, pb, £2.99